Dedicated to:
Clare & Anna

ritten by: Abigail Gartland

Hello, my name is
St. Clare of Assisi

I was born in Italy in 1194.

I loved Jesus ever since I was a little girl.

When I was 15 years old, my father wanted me to get married, but I only wanted to spend my life with Jesus.

Very soon after that, I met a man named Francis. He later became known as St. Francis of Assisi.

He became a mentor
to me and brought m
closer to Jesus.

St. Francis sent me to
ead a group of women
called "The Poor
Clares".

We spent our days depending on Jesus for everything we would need in life.

Every day, we would go out in the world and beg for food, and our other necessities.

We always knew that Jesus would provide for us.

was the leader of our order for 42 years until I died.

I went to Heaven to see Jesus in 1253.

Do you want to be more like me?

You can celebrate my feast day with me on August 11th.

I pray for you every day of your life.

St. Clare of Assisi
pray for us!

About the Author

Abigail Gartland

I love the saints and I love my faith. The idea for sharing the stories of the saints with little ones came when my dear friend were expecting their first baby. I wanted t create something as unique and special as our friendship. Each book is dedicated to very special people and groups who have enriched my faith in different ways. I am blessed to write these stories and appreciate the unending support of my family and friends. When I am not writing am a middle school teacher. I hope you enjoy these stories. I pray for each and every person who opens one of my books to learn more about the saints.

Abbie